PowerKids Readers:

Big Cats

TIGERS

Elizabeth Vogel

The Rosen Publishing Group's
PowerKids Press™
New York

Published in 2002 by The Rosen Publishing Group, Inc.
29 East 21st Street, New York, NY 10010

First Edition

Book Design: Michael Donnellan

Photo Credits: pp.1, 6 © Gail Shumway/FPG International; p.5 © Stan Osolinski/FPG International; p.9 Telegraph Colour Library/FPG International; pp.11, 13, 15 © Mark Newman/International Stock; pp.16, 17 © DigitalVision; p.19 © Maratea/International Stock; p.21 Jeffrey Sylvester/FPG International.

Vogel, Elizabeth.
Tigers / Elizabeth Vogel.
    p. cm. — (Big cats)
Includes bibliographical references (p.   ).and index.
ISBN 0-8239-6020-X (lib. bdg.)
1. Tigers—Juvenile literature. [1. Tigers.] I. Title.
QL737.C23 V643 2002
599.756—dc21

00-013212

Manufactured in the United States of America

2

CONTENTS

Tigers are big cats.
Tigers are the biggest
cats in the world.

Some male
tigers can be as
big as a car.

7

Adult tigers are big, but baby tigers are small. A baby tiger is called a cub.

All tigers have fur.
Their fur is either
orange or white.

Their fur also can
have black stripes.

13

Their stripes allow tigers
to hide in the tall grass.
This helps them hunt
for food.

15

Tigers like to eat meat.
They eat deer or
wild boar.

Tiger cubs watch how their mothers hunt for food. One day they will be big enough to hunt on their own.

19

Tigers also guard their
land from other animals.
They warn the animals
to stay away with
a mighty roar.

WORDS TO KNOW

boar

deer

stripes

Here are more books to read about tigers:

The Big Cats: Lions and Tigers and Leopards
By Jennifer C. Urquehart
National Geographic Society

Tigers
By Don Middleton
Rosen Publishing

To learn more about tigers, check out
this Web site:

www.nationalgeographic.com/tigers/
maina.html

INDEX

Word Count: 123

Note to Librarians, Teachers, and Parents

PowerKids Readers are specially designed to help emergent and beginning readers build their skills in reading for information. Simple vocabulary and concepts are paired with stunning, detailed images from the natural world around them. Readers will respond to written language by linking meaning with their own everyday experiences and observations. Sentences are short and simple, employing a basic vocabulary of sight words, as well as new words that describe objects or processes that take place in the natural world. Large type, clean design, and photographs corresponding directly to the text all help children to decipher meaning. Features such as a contents page, picture glossary, and index help children get the most out of PowerKids Readers. They also introduce children to the basic elements of a book, which they will encounter in their future reading experiences. Lists of related books and Web sites encourage kids to explore other sources and to continue the process of learning.